Karina Champion is a member of Oriel Chambers in Liverpool and the Chair of its Commercial, Chancery and Insolvency Team. She was called to the Bar of England and Wales in 2005, having obtained a degree in Classics from Exeter College, Oxford in 2003 and a Post-Graduate Diploma in Law from The College of Law in 2004. She has over 18 years' experience of representing factoring companies in relation to all aspects of invoice financing litigation and she is considered an expert in her field.

A Practical Guide to Factoring and Invoice Financing

A Practical Guide to Factoring and Invoice Financing

Karina Champion

Barrister, Inner Temple

BA (Hons) (Oxon) Literae Humaniores

Law Brief Publishing

Published 2023 by Law Brief Publishing, an imprint of Law Brief Publishing Ltd
30 The Parks
Minehead
Somerset
TA24 8BT

www.lawbriefpublishing.com

Paperback: 978-1-916698-27-7

To Peter, for opening the doors, and to Natalie, for giving me the courage to walk through them.

PREFACE

Factoring (sometimes known as 'Invoice Financing' or 'Accounts Receivable Financing') is apparently said to have its rudimentary origins in the commercial practices of ancient Mesopotamia, some 5000 years ago.

Today, factoring is both ubiquitous and integral to the world of modern commerce. Surprisingly, however, the subject matter of factoring tends to be perceived as rather arcane from a legal perspective. For obvious reasons (at least to anyone who has ever studied the Law), factoring is rarely, if ever, touched upon at under-graduate degree level and, to the best of the author's knowledge, it is never taught at the stage of professional qualification. Indeed, experience dictates that factoring is an area of commercial law which, rather than actively seeking it out as a field in which to specialise, one tends to fall into by chance (happily, it is submitted).

The aim of this book is to divest the subject of some of its mystery for those readers who are considering dipping their toe into the world of invoice finance litigation (whether they be students of law or established practitioners keen to diversify) and to assist those already practising in the area by providing a straightforward, accessible guide to the practical aspects of factoring as well as the legal principles which underpin it. It is also hoped and envisaged that its contents may be of assistance to those working or aspiring to work in the factoring industry.

In light of the above, it is important to stress that, save insofar as is necessary to enable the reader to understand the modern legal landscape of factoring, this book is not intended to provide the reader with a detailed history and analysis of the origins and evolution of the various legal concepts at play in the field of factoring. Such concepts are legion and comprehensively addressed in various specialist practitioners' texts.

It is equally important to stress that the subject matter of this book is confined to the practice of factoring within the jurisdiction of England and Wales: the laws and customs applicable to factoring in other territories and jurisdictions is without the scope of this book.

The law is stated as it is understood by the author on 22nd November 2023. Insofar as the contents of this book contain any errors or material omissions, whether relating to the law or to modern practices within the factoring industry, any such errors and omissions are the author's own (for which she apologises and which she hopes to correct in the next edition of this book).

This book is not intended to be a substitute for legal advice and readers researching a particular problem or aspect of law should not rely on its contents in isolation but should instead refer to textbooks on the particular aspect of the problem they are researching and to legally qualified professionals where necessary.

I am grateful for the help and assistance of Neil Armstrong of Bibby Financial Services Limited Philip Sheard of Bexley Beaumont Limited and Jonathan Berkson of Bermans Limited. I am also grateful to my family, Chris, James, Eloise and Max, for their love, support and patience.

Karina Champion
November 2023

CONTENTS

CHAPTER ONE

FACTORING

THE TRADITIONAL MODEL

1-01 Factoring, in its traditional form, is a means by which a business ('the Business') is able to accelerate and optimise its cashflow by selling its accounts receivable (referred to variously as 'invoices' or 'debts' herein) to a factoring company ('the Factor') for a discounted price (i.e. for a price less than the face value of the relevant invoice).

1-02 Under the traditional factoring model, the Factor enters into a factoring agreement with the Business pursuant to which the Business assigns to the Factor the unpaid trade invoices it has raised (and will in due course raise) to its customers ('the Customers'). Shortly after the assignment of each such invoice (usually between 1 and 3 working days), the Factor makes an advance payment to the Business (typically somewhere between 75-90% of the invoice value depending on what the parties have agreed), thereby giving the Business accelerated access to funds for which it would ordinarily have had to wait until the expiry of the payment term agreed with its Customer. So, where a Business has payment terms of 30 days from date of invoice, instead of having to wait for 30 days before receiving payment from its Customer, the Business may only have to wait a matter of days (or less than a day in some cases) before receiving the bulk of the funds due under the invoice.

1-03 Depending on the terms of the factoring facility, notice of the fact that the invoice has been assigned to the Factor by the

Business is given to the Customer from whom payment is due (usually when the invoice is raised by means of a written notice printed or stamped on the invoice) and the Customer is informed that the Factor is now the owner of the invoice and payment of the invoice should be made to the Factor rather than the Business. As the assignee and now owner of the Business's unpaid invoices, the Factor takes responsibility for collecting the monies due under the invoices from the Business's Customers. On receipt of payment from those Customers, the Factor then credits the balance of the invoice value to the Business (having first deducted its fees and any other applicable charges).

1-04 The aforesaid process is beneficial for the Business because the Business receives a substantial tranche of the value of its invoice significantly earlier than the invoice falls due for payment from the Customer under the standard payment terms of the Business, thereby improving the Business's cashflow and releasing funds with which to grow the Business. The Business is also able to outsource responsibility for its credit control to the Factor, thereby allowing it to focus on generating further trade.

1-05 The process is obviously beneficial to the Factor as well because the Factor receives the full value of the Business's invoice by way of assignment but is only obliged to pay the Business an agreed proportion of the invoice value, thereby generating a profit.

VARIATIONS AND HYBRIDS

1-06 Not all factoring facilities operate in exactly the same way as the traditional model and it should be stressed that the process described above is only a basic sketch of the fundamental aspects of a traditional factoring facility. There are numerous different permutations of the traditional model such that it is difficult to provide an exhaustive list of all the various types of facilities which exist in modern commerce. As will be seen, this difficulty is compounded by the fact that the nomenclature used to describe different kinds of factoring facilities is not always used consistently, either by lawyers or by those working in the factoring industry.

1-07 It is perhaps useful to start by observing that almost all standard factoring facilities will either be 'Recourse' facilities or 'Non-Recourse' facilities. Equally, almost all standard facilities will either be 'Disclosed' facilities or 'Undisclosed' facilities.

Recourse

1-08 Recourse Factoring is so-called because it allows the Factor to have recourse to the Business in the event that the Customer doesn't pay, or only part-pays, the invoice assigned to the Factor by the Business. If the Customer doesn't pay the Factor or only part-pays the assigned invoice, or if the Customer becomes insolvent, recourse will usually be effected by the Factor requiring the Business to re-purchase the invoice (or so much of it as remains outstanding) from the Factor or by the Factor requiring the Business to indemnify the Factor in respect of non-payment by the Customer. In Recourse Factoring, the Business retains the risk of bad debts. It is for this reason that Recourse Factoring tends to be less expensive than other forms of factoring where it is the Factor, rather than the Business, who bears the majority of the risk of the Business's Customers not paying the Business's invoices.

Non-Recourse

1-09 In Non-recourse Factoring facilities, the Factor takes on the credit risk of the Customer not paying its debts to the Business. Save in certain circumstances (e.g. where there has been a breach of an undertaking or warranty[1] by the Business or where the debt is genuinely disputed by the Customer), the Factor does not have recourse to the Business if invoices are not paid by the Business's Customers, whether by re-assigning them to the Business or seeking an indemnity from the Business in respect of bad debts. It is for this reason that the pre-payment made by the Factor tends to be a lower percentage of the invoice value than in recourse factoring and the Factor's fees[2] tend to be higher.

1-10 In practice, it is rare for a Factor to offer an unconditional, fully non-recourse facility to a Business. Most Factors will usually conduct an assessment of the creditworthiness of the Business's Customers in order to decide upon an appropriate credit limit for each such Customer. Invoices raised by the Business to the Customer will, provided that the Business has complied with its various undertakings and warranties and provided that the relevant invoices are within the credit limit, generally be funded by the Factor on a non-recourse basis. However, the Factor will usually have a right of recourse in respect any invoices raised to the Customer and notified to the

---

1 See at 2-10 and 2-11

2 See Chapter 3

Factor which exceed the applicable credit limit for that particular Customer.

Disclosed

1-11 Traditional factoring facilities tend to be 'Disclosed'. This means that the existence of the facility and the assignment of the Business's invoices to the Factor is made known to the Business's Customers, usually by way of a notice of assignment (in a form prescribed by the Factor) which the Business will stamp or print on each of its invoices before it sends them to the Customers. In practice, most Factors will also send a 'Welcome Letter' (sometimes known as a 'Take-On Letter' or an 'Introductory Letter') to the Business's existing Customers at the outset of the facility and to new Customers as and when they start trading with the Business, informing them of the existence of the facility and giving them notice that all invoices raised by the Business have been or will be (if they do not yet exist) assigned to the Factor and that payment of all such invoices should be made to the Factor (rather than the Business) until further notice.

Undisclosed

1-12 Undisclosed Factoring (often referred to as 'Invoice Discounting' or 'Confidential Factoring') is similar to but different from traditional Disclosed Factoring insofar as the Business's Customers are not informed of the existence of the facility or the fact that the Factor has taken an assignment of the Business's invoices. In practice, this means that (initially at least) the assignment by the Business to the Factor can only take effect in equity. This is because a valid legal assignment under section 36 of the Law of Property Act 1925 requires that written notice of assignment is given to the Business's

Customer. Necessarily, the fact that a facility is undisclosed also means that responsibility for collecting the monies due under the invoices is retained by the Business as (for obvious reasons) the Factor is prohibited from having contact with the Customers in relation to the facility. Once in receipt of monies from a Customer, the Business will remit the gross invoice value to the Factor and the Factor will deduct the value of the advance payment, any accrued interest and its agreed fees. It will then remit the balance of the invoice value to the Business.

1-13 Undisclosed Factoring may appeal to some Businesses who wish to take advantage of the benefits of invoice financing but are concerned that their Customers may not be receptive to the interpolation of the Factor into the existing commercial relationships between themselves and their Customers. For example, where the Business's credit control team generally has a good working relationship with the accounts departments of the Business's Customers, the Business may not wish to jeopardise the good will accrued between the parties by handing over debt recovery to personnel of the Factor with whom the Customer is unfamiliar. Equally, there may be commercially sensitive reasons why a Business might not wish its Customers to be aware that it is using a factoring facility.

1-14 Given that the Factor has no direct contact with the Business's Customers under the terms of an undisclosed factoring facility, the risks to the Factor are inherently greater than where the facility is disclosed to the Customer. For one thing, there is sufficiently more scope for the Business to engage in malpractice, either by inducing the Factor to make advance payments on the basis of fictitious invoices raised by the Business in respect of non-existent transactions (sometimes called 'Fresh-Air Invoicing') or by directing Customers to make payment to an alternative bank account in respect of which the Factor has no control or visibility. The fact that the Factor is unable to make contact with the Business's Customer directly necessarily means that the Factor's opportunities to identify such fraudulent activity are limited. For this reason, undisclosed facilities tend to be offered only to established Businesses with proven credit control infrastructure, high turnover and a healthy credit history.

CHOCC/CHOCS

1-15 CHOCC ('Customer Handles Own Credit Control') or CHOCS ('Customer Handles Own Collections') is a hybrid form of factoring which combines aspects of traditional Disclosed Factoring with aspects of Undisclosed Factoring/Invoice Discounting. It is sometimes also known as 'Disclosed Discounting'. Where the Factor and the Business enter into a CHOCC agreement, the fact that the Business is using a factoring facility is (as per the traditional factoring model) disclosed to the Business's Customer and the Business's invoices will usually be pre-printed/stamped with a notice of assignment requiring the Customer to pay the Factor directly. However, as per the invoice discounting model, the Business retains control of its own debt collection and credit control. Like other forms of factoring, a CHOCC facility may be recourse or non-recourse.

Spot Factoring

1-16 Spot Factoring (also known as 'Selective Invoice Financing') differs from traditional whole turnover/whole ledger factoring insofar as the Business may select only one or several invoices to factor rather than entering into a long-term facility whereby it is obliged to assign all of its present and future invoices to the Factor at the outset of the facility and incur ongoing fees. Generally speaking, the process works in much the same way as traditional whole turnover factoring, with the Factor taking an assignment of the individual invoice/invoices and either assuming responsibility for collecting it/them from the Customers or leaving this for the Business to do. Spot Factoring can be disclosed or undisclosed, recourse or non-recourse.

1-17 Spot Factoring may be of benefit to Businesses whose cashflow is generally healthy but who, for example, may have taken on a long-term contract whereby their Customer is entitled to pay on a staged basis or when all aspects of the Business's obligations have been performed. If, from the Business's perspective, the contract is a large or onerous one in terms of resources and/or initial financial outlay, this can have a significant impact on cashflow and hence the option of Spot Factoring is likely to be an appealing one to a Business in this position. Additionally, some businesses may see it is an advantage that the majority of Factors offering Spot Factoring facilities do not require additional security from the Business in addition to the assignment of the invoice(s) (e.g. personal guarantees and/or all-assets debentures). However, because a Spot Factoring facility is, by definition, a 'one-off' facility with only one or a small number of invoices being financed by the Factor, the Factor's fees tend to be higher than they would be in the context of a long-term facility where the Factor's risk is typically lower.

Reverse Factoring

1-18 Reverse Factoring is a collaborative process involving the Factor, the Business and the Customer. The key difference between Reverse Factoring and the traditional factoring model lies in the fact that it is the Customer, not the Business, who enters into the facility with the Factor. In practice, Reverse Factoring usually works as follows:

- The Business and the Customer enter into a contract/trading relationship whereby the Business agrees to provide goods and/or services to the Customer;
- The Customer enters into an agreement with the Factor pursuant to which the Factor agrees to pay the invoices raised by the Business to the Customer directly to the Business on the Customer's behalf;
- The Business provides the relevant goods and/or services to the Customer and raises an invoice;
- The Customer confirms that the invoice is due and payable and passes it on to the Factor for the Factor to make payment directly to the Business;
- In return for an agreed fee payable to the Factor by the Business (usually deducted by the Factor from the gross invoice value payable to the Business), the Business has the option of calling on the Factor to pay the invoice to the Business within a matter of days (i.e. considerably earlier than the Business's standard payment terms demand), thereby assisting the cashflow of the Business;
- When the invoice matures or often at a later date mutually agreed between the Factor and the Customer, the Customer pays the full value of the invoice to the Factor together with interest.

1-19 Reverse Factoring is still relatively uncommon in the UK as compared with the traditional factoring model whereby the facility is offered by the Factor to the Business rather than the Customer. However, the benefits of Reverse Factoring to all three parties (i.e. Factor, Business and Customer) are easy to recognise. In return for a modest discount on its invoice, the Business is guaranteed payment considerably earlier than its terms would usually permit. In turn, the Customer is able to offer the Business an inexpensive means of accelerated payment, thereby cementing and enhancing its commercial relationship with the Business, with the possibility of negotiating better trading terms than might otherwise have been possible. Furthermore, if the Customer is able to agree extended payment terms with the Factor (i.e. terms more favourable than the Business's standard payment terms), the Customer has longer to pay the invoice and is therefore assisted in terms of its own cashflow. Insofar as the Factor is concerned, it receives a fee from the Business and interest from the Customer on the sums it advances.

Maturity Factoring

1-20 Maturity Factoring differs from traditional factoring insofar as the Factor does not make an advance payment to the Business on assignment of the Business's debts. Instead, the Business assigns its invoice to the Factor and either after an agreed period of days from the date of the invoice ('the Maturity Date') or when the Factor collects the debt from the Customer (whichever is sooner usually), the Factor pays the Business the full notified value of the invoice subject to deduction of its fees.

1-21 The advantage of Maturity Factoring for the Business is the fact it provides the Business with certainty: knowing when and how much it is going to receive on any given date enables the

Business to plan and regulate its cashflow more efficiently. Additionally, where the facility is non-recourse, the risk of bad debt is assumed by the Factor.

Industry-Bespoke Factoring

1-22 Many Factors provide factoring facilities which are bespoke to particular types of Businesses. These tend to be Businesses operating in industries where cashflow is problematic due to a significant time-lag between the delivery of goods/services and the date of payment by their Customers. For example, Employment Businesses which provide temporary workers to their Customers will pay the wages of those workers themselves in the first instance and will then seek reimbursement from their Customers at a later date. Normally the Employment Business will need to pay its workers on a weekly basis whereas, depending on the payment terms agreed with its Customer, it may be anything between 30 and 90 days before the Business receives payment from the Customer. Self-evidently, this time-lag can be problematic in terms of cashflow. For this reason, many Factors offer facilities whereby they will pay the wages of temporary workers directly to those workers on receipt of certified time-sheets (provided by the Business or, in certain circumstances, by the Customer on a self-billing basis) and will then collect payment of the Business's invoices from the Customer at a later date, deducting the advance payments and their fees before crediting the balance to the Business.

CHAPTER TWO

THE FACTORING AGREEMENT

2-01 Whilst different Factors will have their own standard-form agreements, such agreements tend to be relatively formulaic in terms of their content. A typical agreement will, on its face, identify:

1) the Parties (i.e. the Factor and the Business);

2) the basis on and the extent to which debts are/will be assigned from the Business to the Factor (e.g. recourse or non-recourse, disclosed or undisclosed);

3) the Initial Term of the agreement (normally 12 months);

4) the Credit/Funding Limit (if any) extended by the Factor to the Business;

5) the maximum value of any credit note the Business may issue to its Customers;

6) the Pre-payment Percentage (i.e. the percentage of the full value of the Business's invoice which the Factor will pay the Business up-front by way of pre-payment);

7) the Concentration Limit[3];

8) the Factor's various fees and charges[4];

9) the 'Approval Period' for the assigned invoices (i.e. the period of time for which the Factor will allow the assigned invoices to remain unpaid); and

10) the securities the Business will be required to have provided to the Factor prior to the Factor advancing any payment to the Business[5].

2-02 Almost invariably, the agreement will make reference to and append the Factor's standard terms ('the Terms'). Whilst the Terms will differ to some extent depending on the nature of the facility (e.g. recourse or non-recourse, disclosed or undisclosed), there will be a body of standard form clauses contained in all versions of the Terms, irrespective of the precise nature of the facility.

Notification of Debts and Credit Notes

2-03 In whole-turnover facilities, the Business usually agrees that it will assign to the Factor all of its debts (i.e. all of its unpaid trade invoices) in existence at the commencement of the facility as well as those debts which come into existence throughout the duration of the facility. Typically, there will be a carve-out clause excluding invoices raised by the Business which are ineligible for factoring (e.g. pro-forma invoices, invoices payable by cash on delivery, invoices payable to the

---

3 See at 4-12

4 See Chapter 3

5 See Chapter 5

Business by one of its associates and invoices raised by the Business otherwise than in the course of its trade). Such invoices are often called 'Excluded Debts'.

2-04 All non-excluded debts existing at the commencement of the facility will usually be set out in a schedule provided by the Business to the Factor on commencement of the facility and those debts will be assigned by the Business to the Factor by virtue of the express terms of the agreement. The Business will also be required, by virtue of the express terms of the agreement, to provide the Factor with copies of the individual invoices listed in the schedule, copies of all credit notes raised by the Business in relation to those invoices and such other information/documents as may be required by the Factor.

2-05 As regards invoices and credit notes which have not yet come into existence but will come into existence during the lifetime of the facility, the Terms will usually provide that the Business is required to 'notify' the Factor of such invoices and credit notes within a prescribed number of days after the Business has raised them to its Customers, to provide the Factor with copies of such invoices and credit notes and to hold to the Factor's order all documents pertaining to the contract(s) from which the invoices and credit notes arise (e.g. purchase orders, order acknowledgements, delivery notes, statements of account etc). Typically, the Business will notify the Factor of new invoices and credit notes by submitting 'debt schedules' and 'credit note schedules' (in formats prescribed by the Factor) listing all such invoices and credit notes and all such other information as the Factor may require in relation to those invoices and credit notes. Nowadays most Factors have on-line platforms via which the Business is able to upload debt schedules and credit note schedules in real time, thereby expediting pre-payment and optimising cashflow.

2-06 Most facilities will stipulate that on the coming into existence of a non-excluded invoice, ownership of that invoice will be transferred automatically from the Business to the Factor without the need for any further action by the Business or the Factor[6]. However, some facilities may also stipulate that 'notification' by the Business to the Factor of any given debt amounts to deemed written notice by the Business to the Factor that the Business assigns the entirety of the debt to the Factor with full title guarantee and that the Business has complied with all of the undertakings and warranties contained in the Terms insofar as they relate to the relevant debt[7].

Payment by the Factor

2-07 In respect of 'approved' debts (i.e. invoices which the Factor is willing to finance), the Terms will usually provide for a specific period of time within which the Factor is required to make pre-payment to the Business (usually 1-2 days after notification). Equally, they will provide for a specific period of time within which the Factor is required to credit the balance of the debt to the Business once it has received payment from the Business's Customer. Necessarily, the nature of the facility will dictate when payments are to be made by the Factor. Under the terms of a maturity factoring facility, for example, the Factor will not be obliged to make any pre-payment to the Business but (depending on the agreed terms of the facility) the Factor will be obliged to pay the notified value of the invoice to the Business either on the agreed 'Maturity Date' or

---

6 See at 6-13

7 See at 2-10 and 2-11

on (or shortly after) the date on which it receives payment of the debt from the Business's Customer ('the Collection Date').

Charges

2-08 Depending on the nature of the facility, the Terms will dictate the circumstances in which the Factor's charges will be incurred and when payment of those charges must be made by the Business. Normally, a schedule of all of the Factor's various charges will be appended to the written agreement, explaining what and how much they are[8].

Accounting Practices and Procedures

2-09 The Terms will typically contain a set of clauses prescribing the accounting practices and procedures the Factor will use to keep an account of the transactions between the Factor and the Business and the Factor and the Business's Customers.[9] Such clauses may also stipulate the circumstances in which the Factor is entitled to combine the various accounts operated under the facility so as to calculate the overall balance due from the Business to the Factor or from the Factor to the Business.

Undertakings

2-10 Most Terms will contain a set of undertakings which the Business agrees to give to the Factor for the duration of the facility or for so long thereafter as monies remain due and owing to the Factor from the Business. Typically, the Business will be required to promise that:

---

8 See Chapter 3

9 See Chapter 4

- It will comply with all the terms of the facility;
- It will hold on trust any monies it receives in respect of invoices assigned to the Factor and will deliver such monies to the Factor forthwith;
- It will not factor its debts to any third party or otherwise create any security over such debts in favour of a third party;
- It will keep full accounting records;
- It will not vary the payment term allowed to its Customer in respect of any invoice which it has notified to the Factor (i.e. if the payment term agreed between the Business and the Customer is 30 days from date of invoice, the Business will undertake not to vary this by, for example, agreeing to allow the Customer a longer period of time within which to make payment);
- It will not issue any credit note in excess of the agreed credit note limit provided for in the facility;
- It will notify the Factor of:
    - any dispute it has with its Customers;
    - any changes to the creditworthiness of its Customers;

- any changes to its own management and/or control;
- any potential or actual insolvency event (whether in relation to the Business or in relation to any of its Customers).

Warranties

2-11 In addition to the aforesaid undertakings, the Terms will usually contain a series of warranties which the Business is deemed to give to the Factor each and every time it notifies the Factor of a debt. Whilst each Factor's Terms will differ in their specific wording, generally they will contain clauses to the effect that the Business, in respect of each and every debt it notifies to the Factor, warrants that:

- The debt arises from a genuine, legally binding agreement between the Business and its Customer;
- The Business has given the Factor full and accurate details of the agreement;
- The Business has fulfilled all of its obligations in respect of the agreement such that the debt is properly due and owing to the Business by the Customer and there is no known dispute in relation to the debt;
- The debt is one to which the facility applies (i.e. it is not an excluded debt);
- The Customer by whom the debt is owed is solvent;

- The Business has made full and frank disclosure in respect of anything affecting its own solvency.

Notice to Customers

2-12 In a typical disclosed facility, the Terms will set out the obligations of the Business to notify its Customers of the fact that the Business's invoices have been assigned to the Factor. Normally, the Business will be required to give notice of assignment to the Customer by stamping/pre-printing its invoice with a prescribed form of wording informing the Customer that the debt has been assigned to the Factor, that payment should be made to the Factor in accordance with the bank details provided and that only payment to the Factor will amount to good discharge of the debt. Additionally, the Business may be required to write to its existing Customers on the commencement of the facility informing them of the existence of the facility and directing them to make payment to the Factor, until further notice, in respect of all future debts.

Debt Collection

2-13 Depending on the nature of the facility, the Terms will also set out the rights and obligations of both the Factor and the Business as regards collection of debts from the Business's Customers. Where the facility is undisclosed or CHOCC, the Terms will set out the Business's obligations in respect of debt collection and will usually provide that the Factor is not entitled to communicate with the Business's Customer save with the consent of the Business or in the event of any default/breach of the facility by the Business. Clauses which provide for the Business to act as the Factor's agent in respect of debt collection will be of particular importance to the Factor where the facility is undisclosed or where the Factor has the right to appoint the Business to collect debts on the Factor's behalf. Such clauses impose a fiduciary duty on the Business whereby it will typically be required to notify the Factor of any monies it collects on the Factor's behalf, to pay such monies over to the Factor within a specified period of time from receipt and to ensure that all monies collected on behalf of the Factor are kept separately from the Business's own money.

2-14 Equally significant for the Factor and potentially onerous for the Business in traditional disclosed facilities are standard clauses which provide that the Factor is at liberty to collect and/or enforce the payment of debts in whatever manner it sees fit. Such clauses usually provide that the Factor may, in its discretion, settle any debt for less than its notified value, pay the Business's Customer any credit due from the Business to the Customer and take any legal or other action it chooses to enforce a debt against the Business's Customer. It is also common to see clauses which stipulate that the Business is required to abide by any decision of the Factor in terms of debt collection and to assist the Factor where the Factor so requires.

Recourse/Non-Recourse Terms

2-15 The extent to which a Factor may exercise a right of recourse will necessarily depend on the nature of the facility.

2-16 In full recourse facilities, the Terms will usually provide that the Factor may choose to exercise its right of recourse at any time and in any circumstances in respect of any notified debt. In other words, it is entirely within the discretion of the Factor to 'disapprove' an approved debt (and require the Business to pay back the sums advanced in respect of that debt) as and when the Factor sees fit: there need not be any default on the part of the Business or the Business's Customer.

2-17 Most full recourse facilities will also specify that certain events automatically trigger recourse without the need for any election on the part of the Factor (e.g. when the Approval Period for the invoice has expired, when the Customer liable to pay the debt becomes or is at risk of becoming insolvent, when the Business breaches any undertaking or warranty in relation to the debt or when the facility ends).

2-18 When the Factor's right of recourse is engaged (whether by election or automatically) the Terms will usually provide that the Business is obliged immediately to repay the relevant debt (and, if the Factor so demands, all other sums then due and owing to the Factor by the Business). However, depending on the terms of the relevant facility, the Factor may agree with the Business that, when the Approval Period for an invoice comes to an end, the Factor will continue to attempt to collect the debt rather than exercising its right of recourse against the Business straight away. This is known as 'Refactoring' and the Factor will charge the Business a 'Refactoring Fee' at the end of each additional month for which the relevant invoice remains unpaid by the Business's Customer[10].

2-19 When recourse occurs in respect of an invoice, this will usually be effected by the Factor crediting the notified value of the invoice to the Sales Ledger Control Account as disapproved debt. This will reduce the balance of approved debt on the Sales Ledger Control Account, thereby reducing the funds available to the Business.[11]

---

10 See at 3-11 – 3-13

11 See at 4-04, 4-09 and 4-10

2-20 In non-recourse facilities, the terms dictating the circumstances in which the Factor is entitled to exercise a right of recourse are necessarily far more constrained albeit the level of constraint will vary from Factor to Factor. Usually the Factor will only be entitled to exercise a right of recourse against the Business in the event that there has been some of breach of contract on the part of the Business (e.g. a breach of a warranty or undertaking) or the assigned invoice is the subject of a genuine dispute by the Customer.

Termination

2-21 Invariably, the Agreement will specify a 'Minimum Period' for which the facility is to run. The agreed Minimum Period will vary from Factor to Factor and from facility to facility but experience dictates that it will rarely be less than 12 months. During this time, neither party may terminate the facility save (in the case of the Factor) where a 'Termination Event' has occurred. The Agreement will also specify the period of notice the parties will be required to give one another in the event that one of them wishes to terminate the facility after the expiry of the Minimum Period. Again, experience dictates that such notice periods tend to be at least three months.

Termination Events

2-22 The Terms will usually set out a list of events, the occurrence of one or more of which will entitle the Factor to terminate the facility immediately on written notice to the Business. The most common Termination Events are as follows:

- Breach of a warranty or undertaking by the Business;
- Insolvency of the Business;

- Cessation of trade by the Business;
- Change of ownership or control of the Business;
- Failure by the Business to notify the Factor of any new debts coming into existence.

The aforesaid list is not exhaustive. Individual Factors will include various different Termination Events in their Terms depending on the nature of the facility offered to the Business.

Factor's Rights on Termination

2-23 The consequences for the Business of a facility being terminated by reason of a Termination Event can be very serious indeed. In the first instance, most Terms will provide that the Business must immediately pay the Factor all sums owed to the Factor under the agreement. In addition, the Business may be required to re-purchase from the Factor all debts which remain unpaid by the Business's Customers at the date of termination.

Data Protection

2-24 Most written factoring agreements will contain standard-form clauses setting out the Factor's duties and obligations in relation to any personal data collected by the Factor during the course of the parties' relationship. Such clauses will also set out the rights of any individual liable to be affected by the Factor's collection of personal data.

Boilerplate Clauses

2-25 As one would expect, a well-drafted factoring agreement will contain all of the usual boilerplate terms typically found in the standard terms and conditions of a commercial organisation. Such terms will include:

- Clauses specifying the requirements for valid service of notices by either party on the other;
- Clauses providing that all payments the Business is obliged to make to the Factor shall be made without set-off, deduction, abatement, withholding etc;
- Clauses providing that the written factoring agreement is the entire agreement between the Factor and the Business and the Business has not relied, when entering into the agreement, on any prior representations or statements made by the Factor;
- Clauses excluding/limiting liability on the part of the Factor;
- Clauses providing that the Factor will not be deemed to have waived any of its rights on account of any previous indulgence granted to the Business or on account of any previous failure by the Factor to enforce its strict legal rights under the agreement;
- Clauses providing that no variation of the agreement shall be valid unless made in writing and signed by authorised representatives of the Business and the Factor;

- Clauses excluding the rights of third parties to enforce any of the terms of the agreement or exercise any of the rights conferred upon the Factor or the Business by reason of it;

- Clauses dictating the law by which the agreement will be governed (i.e. English Law) and the courts which will have jurisdiction to resolve any dispute between the parties (i.e. the Courts of England and Wales);

- Clauses providing that the invalidity of any clause or part of a clause in the agreement will not render the rest of the agreement or the remaining part of the relevant clause invalid.

CHAPTER THREE

CHARGES AND FEES

3-01 Factoring is rendered profitable to the Factor on account of the various fees charged by the Factor to the Business for the Factor's services. The nature and extent of such fees will vary depending on the type of facility offered by the Factor. For example, the fees charged by the Factor for a full credit-control facility will inevitably be more extensive than those charged by the Factor for a basic invoice discounting facility.

3-02 The standard categories of fees typically charged by most Factors are described below. It should be borne in mind, however, that that the nomenclature used to describe such fees may vary from Factor to Factor.

<u>Set-Up/Arrangement Fee</u>

3-03 Some, but not all, Factors will require the Business to pay a 'Set-Up Fee' (sometimes known as an 'Arrangement Fee') to cover the Factor's administrative costs of preparing the requisite legal documents, undertaking checks regarding the credit history of the Business and its Customers, sending out Welcome Letters (where appropriate) to the Business's Customers and setting up the necessary accounting facilities. Such fees tend to be relatively low (usually between £300 and £500) and it is common for Factors to waive them depending on the anticipated revenue from the facility (amongst other considerations).

Factoring/Service Fee

3-04 The Factoring Fee (sometime known as the 'Service Fee' or the 'Administrative Fee') is a fee typically charged by the Factor to cover its costs of administering the facility on the Business's behalf. It is usually calculated as a fixed percentage of the notified value of each invoice assigned to the Factor by the Business.

3-05 The fixed percentage rate applied to calculate the Factoring Fee will necessarily vary from Factor to Factor and from facility to facility and it will invariably be subject to periodic review. However, as a general rule of thumb, the percentage rates applied in full-service disclosed factoring facilities tend to be somewhere between 0.75% and 2.5% whereas the percentage rates for basic invoice discounting facilities tend to be lower, typically somewhere between 0.2% and 0.5%. The reason for such variance is self-evident. Where a Factor is providing a full-service facility (offering credit control and other ancillary services) the Factor's overheads will necessarily be more significant than they would be if the Factor were simply providing a straightforward invoice discounting facility with the onus being on the Business, rather than the Factor, to collect debts from the Business's customers.

3-06 Most factoring facilities will stipulate that the Business is required to pay the Factor a 'Minimum Fee' per month. So, for example, where the Minimum Fee is £500.00 and the accrued Factoring Fees incurred by the Business only amount to £300.00 at the end of the month, there will be a shortfall of £200.00 which the Factor will debit to the Business's Current Account[12]. Conversely, if the Minimum Fee is £500.00 and

[12] See at 4-05

the accrued Factoring Fees incurred by the Business at the end of the month are £600.00, there will be no shortfall to be debited to the Business's Current Account.

Retrospective Fee

3-07 At the start of a facility, some Factors will charge the Business a fee for taking on the Business's existing ledger (i.e. the existing invoices due and owing to the Business from its Customers which are assigned to the Factor when the facility is incepted). Normally, this 'Retrospective Fee' (as it is commonly called) will be calculated by reference to the same percentage rate as the Factoring Fee. So, if the value of the existing ledger is e.g. £100,000.00 when the facility is incepted and the Retrospective Fee is 5%, the Business would pay the Factor a one-off fee of £5,000.00 in return for the Factor taking on the Business's existing ledger.

Discount Charge

3-08 The Discount Charge is the fee charged by the Factor to the Business in return for the Factor making advance payments against the Business's invoices. Albeit completely different, it is in many ways akin to the interest charged by a creditor to a borrower in respect of a loan.

3-09 Most Factors calculate and apply their Discount Charge on a daily basis by reference to the 'Funds in Use' (i.e. the debit balance due on the Business's Current Account at the end of each day)[13]. At the end of each day, the Funds in Use will be multiplied by the Factor's agreed Discount Rate (which is usually between 1 and 5% above a specified bank base rate).

---

13 See at 4-08

This calculation will produce an annual discount which is then divided by 365 (or 366 in a leap year) to give a daily discount. So, for example, if the discount rate is 3% above base rate, the prevailing base rate is 2% and the Funds in Use are £100,000.00 at the end of the relevant day, the Discount Charge applied by the Factor will be £13.70 (i.e. £100,000.00 x 0.05/365).

3-10 The applicable Discount Rate will vary from Factor to Factor and from facility to facility and (like the Factoring Fee) it will be subject to periodic review by the Factor. Typically, however, the greater the size and cumulative value of the invoices assigned by the Business to the Factor, the more favourable the Discount Rate is likely to be to the Business.

Refactoring Fee

3-11 Almost all factoring facilities will specify an 'Approval Period' (sometimes known as a 'Credit Period') for invoices assigned by the Business to the Factor. The Approval Period is the period of time within which the Factor expects the Customer to pay the invoice and it will typically vary from 30 to 90 days, starting from the date on which the invoice is raised by the Business to the Customer.

3-12 If an invoice is not paid by the Business's Customer during the Approval Period, most recourse facilities will provide that the Factor is entitled to exercise recourse against the Business in respect of the unpaid invoice. As stated above, however, rather than exercising recourse immediately, the Factor will often agree to refactor the debt. In these circumstances, the Factor will be entitled to charge the Business a 'Refactoring Fee'.

3-13 In practice, the Refactoring Fee will usually be calculated on the balance of the invoice outstanding on the last day of each month, starting with the month in which the initial Approval Period expires. So, for example, if the agreed Refactoring Fee is 2%, the notified value of the invoice is £10,000.00, the Approval Period expires on 15 June and the full notified value of the invoice remains outstanding on 30 June, the Factor will be entitled to charge the Business a Refactoring Fee of £200.00 (i.e. 2% of £10,000.00) on 30 June. Equally, if the outstanding balance of the invoice is £5,000.00 on 31 July (the Customer having made a part-payment of £5,000.00 in the meantime), the Factor will be entitled to charge the Business a Refactoring Fee of £100.00 on 31 July (i.e. 2% of £5,000.00).

Review Fee

3-14 Some Factors will include a Review Fee in their facilities. This tends to be a small fee payable on each anniversary of the facility (typically not more than £500.00) to cover the Factor's costs of reviewing the facility and revising the applicable fees where appropriate.

Credit Note Fee

3-15 Where the Business is obliged to raise a credit note against the value of a notified invoice, the Factor may (depending on the terms of the facility) charge the Business a Credit Note Fee, usually calculated as an agreed percentage of the notified value of the credit note. The primary purpose of this fee is to compensate the Factor for the administrative costs involved with processing a credit note from an accounting perspective.

Trust Account Fee

3-16 Where the Factor and the Business enter into a non-disclosed facility, the Business's Customers will (for obvious reasons) not be directed to make payment of the Business's invoices directly to a bank account in the name of the Factor. However, most Factors will wish to have some level of control over and/or access to the bank account into which those Customers do make payments to the Business. For this reason, the Factor will often set up a bank account in the Business's name to which the Factor has access and over which it has control. The cost of maintaining such an account will typically be charged back to the Business by the Factor, usually as a percentage of the payments made into the account each month.

Disbursements

3-17 Depending on the nature of the facility provided by the Factor, certain expenses may be incurred by the Factor which it is entitled to re-charge to the Business. For example, some Factors will offer a CHAPS service whereby payments requested by the Business are made by the Factor on the same day. This will incur a fee with the Factor's bank which, pursuant to the agreed terms of the facility, the Factor is entitled to re-charge to the Business.

CHAPTER FOUR

ACCOUNTING PRACTICES

4-01 To the untrained (and sometimes even the trained) eye, the accounting practices and procedures adopted by most Factors can be difficult immediately to fathom. However, for a practitioner regularly engaged in factoring litigation, a good working knowledge of such practices and procedures will be invaluable, not least because the Court will often be unfamiliar with such practices and procedures and may require assistance in understanding how the sums in dispute have been calculated by the Factor.

4-02 Different Factors may use slightly different accounting practices and procedures and this chapter is by no means intended to provide an exhaustive survey of all such practices and procedures as exist within the industry. Instead, the matters discussed below are intended to give an overview of the accounting practices and procedures which tend, in the writer's experience, to be those most commonly employed by Factors at the time of writing.

4-03 Broadly speaking, the majority of Factors tend to maintain two tandem accounts when operating a standard factoring facility. Whilst different Factors may refer to these accounts by different names and manage them slightly differently, the function of each such account is broadly the same. For the purposes of this book, the two accounts will be identified as follows: 1) the Sales Ledger Control Account; and 2) the Current Account.

4-04 Some Factors will also keep what is effectively a notional account which records what the Factor would owe the Business if the entirety of the debt notified by the Business to the Factor were to be collected in by the Factor and any debit balance on the Current Account were to be fully paid off by the Business. This is sometimes known as the 'Client Account'.

Sales Ledger Control Account

4-04 The Sales Ledger Control Account (which is sometimes also known as the 'Debtors Control Account') is an account operated by the Factor in the name of the Business. When the Business assigns an invoice to the Factor, the notified value of the invoice (if approved by the Factor) will be recorded in the Sales Ledger Control Account as a debit. If and when invoices are subsequently disapproved by the Factor or if the Business raises a credit notice to a Customer which diminishes the value of an approved invoice, the amount of any such disapproval or credit note will be entered as a credit in the Sales Ledger Control Account, thereby reducing the amount of approved debt. Equally, as and when collections are made by the Factor from the Business's Customers, the amounts received by the Factor from the Customers will be entered onto the Sales Ledger Control Account as a credit, also reducing the amount of approved debt. The debit balance on the Sales Ledger Control Account at any given time therefore represents the amount of approved debt purchased by the Factor from the Business which remains unpaid by the Business's Customers.

Current Account

4-05 The Current Account is a running account in which the Factor records all transactions between the Factor and the Business, the resulting balance of which will represent either what the

Business owes to the Factor or what the Factor owes to the Business as the case may be.

4-06 When a pre-payment is made to the Business by the Factor in respect of an approved notified invoice, this will be recorded as a debit in the Current Account. The Factor's Factoring Fee and any other fees payable by the Business to the Factor will also be recorded as debits in the Current Account as and when they are charged by the Factor. When collections are made by the Factor from the Business's Customers, the value of those collections will be recorded as a credit in the Current Account.

4-07 By way of a basic worked example, let us suppose that: 1) the Business assigns an invoice to the Factor with a notified value of £1,000.00; 2) the agreed pre-payment percentage is 80%; and 3) the agreed Factoring Fee is 5% of the notified value of each invoice. In this scenario:

- The Factor will make a pre-payment of £800.00 to the Business (i.e. 80% of £1,000.00). This will be entered as a debit of £800 on the Current Account;

- The Factor's Factoring Fee is £50 (i.e. 5% of £1,000). The sum of £50 will also be entered as a debit on the current account, meaning that the cumulative debit balance will be £850.00;

- Subsequently, the Factor makes a collection of £600.00 from the Customer. The Factor will credit this sum to the Current Account, leaving a debit balance of £250.00 (i.e. a balance of £250.00 owed by the Business to the Factor).

4-08 The Factor's Discount (which is usually calculated on a daily basis and entered as a debit on the Current Account) is calculated by taking the debit balance (if any) on the current account (i.e. the Funds in Use) at the end of each day and multiplying this by the agreed discount rate. So, for example, if the debit balance is £250.00 at the end of the day, the agreed discount rate is 3% above base rate and the prevailing base rate is 2%, the Factor will multiply £250.00 by 5% to produce an annual discount (i.e. £250 x 0.05 = £12.50). Assuming that the Factor calculates the daily discount by dividing the annual discount by 365, this will result in a Factor's discount of £0.03 for the day in question (i.e. £12.50/365 = £0.03). The discount of £0.03 will be then debited against the current account, leaving a debit balance of £250.03 owed by the Business to the Factor at the beginning of the following day.

Availability

4-09 The issue uppermost in the minds of most Businesses will be the availability of funds (i.e. the amount of funds available for the Business to draw down on as and when such funds are needed). 'Availability', put simply, is the difference between the amount of approved debt on the Sales Ledger Control Account and the balance of the Current Account (less any sums which the Factor has elected to hold in reserve for contingencies).

4-10 So, by way of crude example, if the amount of approved debt on the Sales Ledger Control Account is £1,000.00 and the debit balance on the Current Account is £1,500.00, this will mean that there is Availability (sometimes called 'Entitlement') of -£500.00. In other words, there are no available funds for the Business to draw down on. Conversely, if the amount of approved debt on the Sales Ledger Control

Account is £2,000.00 and the debit balance on the Current Account is £1,500.00, the availability will be £500 because the overall state of account is that the Factor owes the Customer £500. If there is a credit balance on the Current Account, the available funds will be the total of the amount in credit and the approved debt on the Sales Ledger Control Account (less any sums which the Factor has elected to hold in reserve for contingencies).

Credit Limit

4-11 Most Factors will agree a Credit Limit (sometimes known as a 'Funding Limit') with the Business. The amount of the Credit Limit will normally be stated on the face of the factoring agreement but it may be reviewed from time to time at the Factor's discretion. In essence, the Credit Limit is the maximum debit balance ('funds in use') the Factor will permit on the current account (the debit balance being the amount the Business owes to the Factor).

Concentration Limit

4-12 Most factoring agreements will stipulate a 'Concentration Limit' (sometimes known as an 'Approval Limit' or simply as 'High Involvement'). The Concentration Limit is the maximum percentage of the total unpaid approved debt on the Sales Ledger Control Account (i.e. the total amount of unpaid debt cumulatively due from all of the Business's Customers) against which the Factor will make pre-payments in respect of any individual Customer of the Business. So, for example, if the Concentration Limit is 30% and the total amount of unpaid debt on the Sales Ledger Control Account is £100,000.00, the Factor will only fund pre-payments of £30,000.00 in respect of invoices due from any individual

Customer of the Business. In the event that the Business notifies the Factor of invoices which cause the total unpaid debt of an individual Customer to exceed the Concentration Limit, those invoices will not be pre-paid by the Factor.

4-13 So, if the total unpaid debt on the Sales Ledger Control Account is £100,000.00 and £50,000.00 of this sum is due from one individual Customer of the Business, the total unpaid debt in respect of which the Factor will make pre-payments is £80,000.00 (i.e. £50,000.00 in respect of unpaid debt attributable to other Customers and £30,000.00 in respect of the individual Customer whose unpaid debt exceeds the Concentration Limit). If the pre-payment percentage is 80%, this means that the Business will only be entitled to pre-payments of £64,000.00 (i.e. 80% of £80,000.00). Conversely, if the Concentration Limit hadn't been exceeded, the Business would be entitled to pre-payments of £80,000.00 (i.e. 80% of £100,000.00).

Reports

4-14 Nearly all Factors now operate online platforms on which and from which the Business can view and download a multiplicity of different reports capturing the state of play at any given time between the Business and the Factor and between the Factor and the Business's Customers. Of particular importance to the Business are 'Availability Reports': these enable the Business to ascertain the extent of the funds available for drawdown by the Business at any given time.

CHAPTER FIVE

SECURITIES

5-01 Save in the case of most spot factoring facilities, it is customary for the Factor to require the Business to provide certain securities in addition to the quasi-security created by the assignment of the debts notified by the Business to the Factor. Typically, the securities the Factor will insist upon are personal and/or corporate guarantees/indemnities and 'all-assets' debentures.

GUARANTEES AND INDEMNITIES

5-02 It will almost always be a requirement of a Factor entering into a facility with a Business that the obligations of the Business are secured by way of a personal guarantee and indemnity from an individual or individuals closely connected with the Business[14].

5-03 If the Business is a limited company, it will usually be the director or directors (if there are more than one) of the Business who will be called on by the Factor to give a personal guarantee and indemnity. In certain circumstances, the Factor may also require a corporate guarantee from a parent or associated company of the Business. If the Business is an incorporated partnership (i.e. an LLP), the Factor will usually require that guarantees and indemnities are given by the

---

[14] Save in the case of Spot Factoring

designated members of the partnership[15]. In the case of unincorporated partnerships and sole traders, a personal guarantee and indemnity will not be required as those entities will be personally liable for any financial obligations owed by the Business to the Factor in any event.

5-04 The law relating to guarantees and indemnities is not without its significant complexities and a full analysis of the principles involved is without the scope of this book. However, by way of basic overview, a guarantee in the context of factoring is a promise by the Guarantor to be answerable for the financial obligations of the Business to the Factor if the Business defaults in relation to those obligations. Under the terms of a guarantee, the Guarantor is a 'secondary obliger' who may only be called upon to pay the debts of the Business if the Business ('the primary obliger') is in default. Conversely, under the terms of an indemnity, the Guarantor is himself a primary obligor whose obligation it is to hold the Factor harmless against any (otherwise irrecoverable) losses the Factor might suffer by virtue of the Business's failure to discharge its financial obligations.

5-05 The key (but not the only) differences between a guarantee and an indemnity are:

- A guarantee (or some memorandum or note of it) must be made in writing and signed by the Guarantor or a person authorised by the Guarantor[16]. Conversely, an indemnity need not be made in writing and it need not

15 See Section 8 of the Limited Liability Partnership Act 2000

16 Section 4 of the Statute of Frauds 1677

be signed by the Indemnifier or a person authorised by him;

- Because a guarantee imposes a secondary obligation on the Guarantor (i.e. an obligation which is contingent upon the primary obligation of the Business), the liability of the Guarantor is considered to be co-extensive with that of the Business, meaning that anything which discharges the Business from its liability to the Factor will generally (but not without exception) also discharge the Guarantor from his liability to the Factor. This is not the case with an indemnity: because the Indemnifier's obligation to the Factor is a primary obligation, it will remain enforceable against him even when the Business is discharged from its own obligations.

5-06 In light of the above, it is important from the Factor's point of view that an individual called upon to be a Guarantor actually executes a document which incorporates both a valid guarantee and a valid indemnity. The fact that a document is described on its face as being a 'Guarantee and Indemnity' does not necessarily mean that it is so. It is imperative, therefore, that the actual wording of the document is sufficiently clearly drafted so as to render the Guarantor liable to the Factor both as 'secondary obligor' (i.e. by means of guarantee) and as 'primary obligor' (i.e. by means of indemnity). In practice, most well-drafted guarantee and indemnity documents used by Factors will contain distinct and separate promises identifying the Guarantor's obligation both as guarantor and as indemnifier.

Nature of Guarantee

5-07 The Factor will invariably want to ensure that the guarantee obtained from the Guarantor is an 'all-monies' guarantee rather a guarantee relating to a specific transaction or transactions. It is therefore imperative that the terms of the guarantee explicitly provide for the Guarantor to be answerable for **all future** obligations of the Business to the Factor as well as all existing ones. If the guarantee does not stipulate that the Guarantor is so liable, there is a risk that the Court will deem the Guarantor's obligations to be confined only to those existing at the time the guarantee was executed. As such, any financial obligations the Business subsequently incurs to the Factor will be outside the scope of the Guarantor's obligations.

5-08 In practice, most Factors will seek to ensure that the definition of 'Guaranteed Liabilities' (sometimes called 'Secured Liabilities') is sufficiently widely drafted in the guarantee so as to include (by way of example only): all present and future monies, obligations and liabilities due and owing to the Factor by the Business, whether actual or contingent, whether owed jointly or severally, whether owed by the Business as principal or surety or in any other capacity, and whether arising under the facility (or any variation of it) or under any future facility, contract, agreement or arrangement between the Business and the Factor.

Extent of Guarantee

5-09 The Factor will usually require the Guarantor to provide either a 'limited' or an 'unlimited' all-monies guarantee, the former being a guarantee in respect of all of the Business's financial obligations to the Factor without limit as to amount and the latter being a guarantee and indemnity in respect of all the Business's financial obligations to the Factor up to a specified monetary limit. Which type of guarantee the Factor requires will depend on the practice of the Factor, the nature of the Business and the perceived financial risk of the facility to the Factor.

5-10 Under the terms of a limited guarantee, the guarantor usually agrees to guarantee all the financial obligations of the Business under the facility but only up to a certain, specified amount. If there is more than one guarantor, the guarantee will usually specify whether the agreed amount applies to each Guarantor individually or whether it applies to them cumulatively. For example, if the specified financial limit is £200,000.00 and there are four Guarantors, they may be liable to the Factor for a maximum of £200,000.00 each or they may be cumulatively liable for a maximum of £200,000.00 and to the extent that one of them pays more than his pro-rata share (i.e. more than £50,000.00) he will (in theory) be able to call on his co-guarantors for reimbursement of the amount by which he has overpaid.

Consideration

5-11 Guarantees and indemnities are contracts like any other contracts and for this reason the usual requirements for a binding contract will apply (i.e. the need for offer and acceptance, an intention to create legal relations, consideration etc). In practice, most Factors ensure that the guarantees and indemnities they obtain from Guarantors are made by deed so as to ensure that the question of consideration is never in issue. However, it is not unknown for mishaps to occur whereby what was intended to be a deed fails to meet the criteria for a validly executed deed such that the agreement takes effect only as a simple contract. Whilst consideration moving from the Factor to the Guarantor can usually be inferred from the circumstances of the transaction, most Factors tend to take the precaution of including a preamble which states that the Guarantor has agreed to provide the relevant guarantee and indemnity in consideration for the Factor agreeing to provide/agreeing to continue to provide factoring services to the Business.

DEBENTURES

5-12 Where the Business is a limited company or an LLP, the Factor is likely to require that the Business executes an all-assets debenture in favour of the Factor as security for the Business's financial obligations to the Factor. A debenture of this nature will usually be required in addition to any personal and/or corporate guarantees the Factor obtains from the directors/designated partners/associated companies of the Business.

5-13 Under the terms of a standard all-assets debenture, the Business will typically be required to grant the Factor:

i. A first legal mortgage over all of its existing interests and estates in any real property;

ii. fixed charges over:

   - all interests and estates in real property acquired by the Business in the future;

- all present and future interests of the Business in any real property which are not effectively mortgaged or otherwise charged;

- all present and future rights, licences, guarantees, rents, deposits, contracts, covenants and warranties held by the Business in relation to any real property;

- all present and future goodwill and uncalled capital of the Business;

- all plant, machinery and equipment of the Business;

- all Intellectual Property of the Business;

- all Book Debts of the Business;

- all of the shares and securities held by the Business;

- all monies standing to the credit of the Business's accounts with any bank or other financial institution from time to time.

iii. A first floating charge over all of the Business's undertaking, property, assets and rights not otherwise effectively mortgaged, charged or assigned to the Factor.

5-14 The legal issues encountered in the drafting, implementation and enforcement of all-assets debentures are numerous and so vast in scope that a comprehensive survey of the same would justify an entire book in its own right. Practitioners researching any particular legal point relating to debentures would be well advised to consult specialist texts pertaining to Securities.

CHAPTER SIX

ASSIGNMENT

6-01 The mechanism which underpins factoring and invoice discounting facilities is the assignment of invoices by the Business to the Factor. Assignment of an invoice may either be effected in law ('Legal Assignment') or in equity ('Equitable Assignment').

LEGAL ASSIGNMENT

6-02 A Legal Assignment (also known as a 'Statutory Assignment') is an assignment which is made in accordance with section 136(1) of the Law of Property Act 1925. Section 136(1) of the Law of Property Act 1925 provides that:

> "*Any absolute assignment by writing under the hand of the assignor (not purporting to be by way of charge only) of any debt or other legal thing in action, of which express notice in writing has been given to the debtor, trustee or other person from whom the assignor would have been entitled to claim such debt or thing in action, is effectual in law (subject to equities having priority over the right of the assignee) to pass and transfer from the date of such notice—*
>
> *(a) the legal right to such debt or thing in action;*
>
> *(b) all legal and other remedies for the same; and*
>
> *(c) the power to give a good discharge for the same without the concurrence of the assignor....*"

6-03 In order to take effect as a legal assignment pursuant to section 136(1) of the Law of Property Act 1936, the purported assignment must therefore meet the following criteria:

i. It must be absolute (and not be made by way of charge only);

ii. It must be made in writing under the hand of the assignor;

iii. Express notice of the assignment must have been given to the party liable to pay the invoice.

Absolute Assignment

6-04 In order to take effect as a Legal Assignment, the assignment of an invoice from the assignor to the assignee must be '*absolute*'. This means that the assignment must transfer complete and unconditional ownership of the entire invoice to the assignee together with all rights and interests incidental to such ownership. An assignment of only part of an invoice will not amount to an absolute assignment within the meaning of section 136(1) of the Law of Property Act 1925. Equally, if the assignor merely grants the assignee a charge over the invoice, this will be insufficient to amount to an absolute assignment as the assignor will still retain ownership over the invoice, subject to the security created in favour of the assignee by virtue of the charge.

In Writing

6-05 For the purposes of section 136, '*writing*' includes typing, printing, lithography, photography and other modes of representing or reproducing words in a visible form.[17] There is no prescribed form of writing that an assignment must take and it need not be made by Deed. In the context of factoring, the assignment will invariably be in writing and notwithstanding that there is no requirement for it to be made by deed, it almost always will be in practice.

Under the Hand of the Assignor

6-06 For an assignment to be made "*under the hand of the assignor*" it must bear the assignor's signature (which can include his initials or his mark[18]). The assignment need not also be signed by the assignee in order to be effective. It seems likely, (albeit there is no direct authority on the point) that a digital signature would suffice for the purposes of section 136(1) of the Law of Property Act 1925.

17 See Section 5 and Schedule 1 of the Interpretation Act 1978

18 See Electronic Rentals Pty Ltd v Anderson (1971) HCA 13 at [18]: "*But when a document is required by statute to be under a man's hand or signed by him what is ordinarily meant is that he must personally sign it, with his name or his mark, by a pen or by a stamp*"

Notice of Assignment

6-07 By virtue of section 196(1) of the Law of Property Act 1925[19], notice of assignment must be in writing and it can be given to the Customer at any time[20] by the Business, by the Factor or by any third party acting with the authority of either the Business or the Factor. The requirement for writing is strict even if the debtor is not able to read[21].

6-08 Notice of assignment need not take any prescribed form provided that it is sufficient to convey to the Customer that the relevant invoice has been assigned to the Factor and that payment of the invoice must be made to the Factor rather than the Business. This was clarified in Van Lynn Developments Ltd v Pelias Construction Co Ltd[22] wherein Widgery LJ stated at 615:

> "*The section does not speak of "a notice": it speaks of "notice." Accordingly, it is wrong to suppose that a separate document purposely prepared as a notice, and described as such, is necessary in order to satisfy the statute. The statute only requires that information relative to the assignment shall be conveyed to the debtor, and that it shall be conveyed in writing.*"

---

19 Section 196(1) of the Law of Property Act 1925 provides that: "*Any notice required or authorised to be served or given by this Act shall be in writing.*"

20 See Bateman v Hunt [1904] 2 K.B. 530 at 538: "*The statute prescribes no limit of time within which notice must be given, nor does it lay down that the notice must be given by any particular person; and we can see no good ground for holding that the notice given by the plaintiffs was ineffectual.*"

21 See Hockley v Goldstein (1920) 90 L.J. K.B. 111.

22 [1969] 1 Q.B. 607

6-09 Whilst a notice of assignment should make clear to the debtor that the relevant invoice has been assigned by the assignor to the assignee and that the debtor should pay the assignee (as opposed to the assignor), it is not necessary for the notice of assignment to state the date on which the invoice was assigned from the assignor to the assignee nor it is fatal to the validity of a notice that it erroneously asserts that notice has previously been given when, in fact, it has not[23]. However, if the notice does identify a date of assignment and it transpires that the identified date is incorrectly stated, it has been held that the notice is invalid[24]. This is because a notice which refers to an assignment which took place e.g. on 5 February 2023 (when, in fact, the assignment actually took place on 6 February 2023) purports to give notice of an assignment which never took place and fails to give notice of the assignment which did take place. Given that section 136(1) of the Law of Property Act 1925 does not require that a notice of assignment should state the date of assignment, it is submitted that a Factor wishing to avoid the possibility of a notice being deemed invalid may consider it prudent not to refer to the date of the assignment at all in the notice.

6-10 In the context of disclosed factoring, the Factor will usually require that each invoice sent out to a Customer by the Business is stamped or pre-printed with a notice of assignment in a form prescribed by the Factor. Typically such notice will take the following form:

---

23 Van Lynn Developments Ltd. v Pelias Construction Co. Ltd. (Formerly Jason Construction Co. Ltd.) [1969] 1 Q.B. 607

24 W. F. Harrison & Co. Ltd. v Burke [1956] 1 W.L.R. 419

'The amount due under this invoice has been assigned and must be paid to [the Factor, Factor's address]. Only payment to [the Factor] will give good discharge for the debt."

6-11 On the inception of a disclosed facility, the Factor may also send out a 'Welcome Letter' (sometimes known as a 'Take On Letter' or an 'Introductory Letter') to all existing and prospective Customers of the Business, informing those Customers that all unpaid invoices previously raised by the Business have been assigned to the Factor and that, until further notice, all invoices raised by the Business in the future will also be assigned to the Factor such that only payment to the Factor will give the Customer good discharge for the debt created thereby.

6-12 It is important to note that an invoice which has not yet been raised can only amount to a future chose in action and a future chose in action (i.e. a chose in action which does not yet exist) cannot be the subject of an immediate assignment[25]. As such, the Business's promise to assign all future trade invoices to the Factor is merely an agreement to assign, not an actual assignment, and therefore it must be supported by valuable consideration moving from the Factor to the Business.

6-13 An agreement by the Business to assign a future invoice will automatically give rise to an equitable assignment of the invoice to the Factor as soon as the invoice comes into existence and neither the Business nor the Factor need do anything further to effect such an assignment. However, in order to ensure that the assignment becomes a legal assignment (rather than one which merely takes effect in equity), notice of the assignment will need to be given to the Business's

25 Williams v Atlantic Assurance Co Ltd [1933] 1 K.B. 81 at 106

Customer. In the circumstances, whilst a 'Welcome Letter' will generally amount to valid notice of assignment in respect of debts already in existence when the letter is sent out, it will not suffice to give notice of assignment in respect of future invoices in circumstances where valid notice of an assignment cannot be given before the assignment has actually been made.

EQUITABLE ASSIGNMENT

6-14 Any assignment of an invoice by the Business to the Factor which does not comply with the criteria set out in section 136 Law of Property Act 1925 is likely to take effect as an Equitable Assignment.

6-15 An Equitable Assignment need not be in writing and notice of such assignment need not be given to the Customer. Indeed, in cases of undisclosed factoring facilities, it is imperative that notice of assignment is not given to the Customer.

6-16 Whilst a Factor who has taken a statutory assignment of a debt owed to the Business by a Customer can bring proceedings against the Customer in his own name and without needing to join the Business as a party to the proceedings, a factor who only takes an assignment in equity, whilst entitled to sue in his own name because he is beneficially entitled to the debt[26], may nevertheless be required to join the Business to the proceedings.

6-17 The underlying rationale for requiring that the Business is joined as a party to the proceedings is to protect the Customer from facing successive claims from both the Factor and the Business in respect of the same debt. If the assignment fails to

[26] See Bexhill UK Ltd v Razzaq [2012] EWCA Civ 1376

comply with section 136(1) of the Law of Property Act 1936 because it is not an absolute assignment, this means that the Business has not fully divested itself of its interest in the debt and hence the Customer may be at risk of being sued both by the Factor and by the Business. Ensuring that all claims against the Customer are finalised in one set of proceedings to which the Factor and the Business are both parties is therefore desirable. However, if the assignment fails to comply with section 136(1) of the Law of Property Act 1936 merely because the Customer has not been given notice of assignment and there is no argument that the Business has retained some form of interest in the debt, there is no practical purpose to be served by the Business being joined to the proceedings. This was most recently reiterated in the case of *Mailbox (Birmingham) Ltd v Galliford Try Construction Ltd*[27] wherein O'Farrell J stated at [50]:

> "*Where there has been an assignment that takes effect in equity, the general rule is that it is the equitable assignee who has the right to sue because the equitable assignee is beneficially entitled to the thing in action: Bexhill v Razzaq (above) per Aikens LJ at Para.58. Although it is open to the court to require an assignor under an equitable assignment to be joined to any proceedings to enforce the assigned rights, this is a procedural requirement so as to bind the assignor and protect the debtor from a second claim. Where, as in this case, there is no dispute between assignor and assignee as to the effect of the assignment, and therefore no risk of a further claim in respect of the assigned rights, it is not necessary for the assignor to be joined.*"

27 [2017] EWHC 67 (TCC)

6-18 In the context of factoring, it will usually be the case that an assignment which fails to satisfy the criteria set out in section 136 of the Law Property Act 1925 does so because the Customer has not been provided with notice of assignment. For obvious reasons, cases in which the assignment fails to be statutory because it is not absolute or because it has not been made in writing signed under the hand of the Business are comparatively rare. Nevertheless, it is surprisingly common for Customers defending claims brought by Factors for non-payment of assigned invoices to argue that because they have never received notice of assignment, the assignment can only take effect in equity and hence the Factor's claim is defective (or even abortive) because the Business has not been joined as a party to the proceedings. It is submitted that this betrays a fundamental misunderstanding of the rationale behind the joinder of the assignor in cases of equitable assignment.

RESTRICTIONS ON ASSIGNMENT

6-19 If the Business happens to be trading with a Customer on the basis of the Customer's standard terms and conditions of business rather than on its own standard terms and conditions of business, it is possible that the Customer's terms might contain a clause purporting to prohibit the Business from assigning its receivables (i.e. the invoices it raises to the Customer), either without the consent of the Customer or, in some cases, under any circumstances at all.

6-20 Pursuant to regulation 2(1) of The Business Contract Terms (Assignment of Receivables) Regulations 2018, any term of a contract entered into after 31 December 2018 will (save in certain limited circumstances) have no effect to the extent that the term prohibits or imposes a condition, or other restriction, on the assignment of a receivable arising under the contract or any other contract between the same parties. The limited circumstances in which such a term will have effect are set out in regulations 3 and 4. In summary, regulation 3 provides that the relevant term **will** have effect where the supplier (i.e. the Business in the context of factoring) is a large enterprise or a special purpose vehicle and regulation 4 provides that the term will have effect where the contract is of a particular type listed therein.

6-21 It is submitted that a significant number of Businesses either utilising factoring services or seeking to enter into factoring facilities in the future will be able to avail themselves of the regulations insofar as their Customers' terms contain clauses purporting to prohibit assignment of receivables. However, it should not be assumed that this will always be the case and reference should be made to regulations 3 and 4 in the event of doubt.

THE IMPORTANCE OF NOTICE OF ASSIGNMENT

6-22 As discussed above[28], it is an essential feature of undisclosed factoring facilities that the Business's Customers remain unaware of the facility and the fact that the debts which they owe (or will in the future owe) to the Business have been assigned to the Factor. This means that (at least while the facility is operating well and the parties are complying with their obligations to one another) no notice of assignment will be given to the Business's Customers. Aside from the risks that this presents to the Factor in terms of the potential for

[28] See at 1-13

fraudulent activity by the Business[29], the inability of the Factor to give notice of assignment to the Business's Customers or to procure that such notice is given by the Business, has other significant implications for the Factor as well.

6-23 One of the consequences of providing the Customer with notice of assignment is that the Customer will be prevented from raising a defence of independent set-off against a claim brought by the Factor unless the debt or other cause of action giving rise to the set-off had accrued ***prior*** to the date on which the Customer was given notice of assignment[30]. As such, a Factor who is prevented from giving notice of assignment (or from procuring that notice of assignment is given by the Business) to the Customer is unable to limit its exposure to the risk of the Customer raising a defence of independent set-off against any claim the Factor might bring against the Customer.

6-24 Another consequence of not giving notice of assignment is that if the Business should induce the Customer to make payment otherwise than into the bank account mutually agreed between the Factor and the Business as being the designated bank account for all collections made by the Business on the Factor's behalf, the Factor will have no means of pursuing the Customer for payment of the debt and will have to pursue the Business instead. Conversely, where a Customer has received notice that a debt has been assigned to the Factor and the Customer disregards such notice and proceeds to pay the debt

[29] See at 1-14

[30] See at 7-12 and 7-13

to the Business instead, the Factor will be able to compel the Customer to pay the debt again, this time to the Factor[31].

6-25 Finally, whilst is it not a common occurrence, problems may also be encountered if the Business assigns to the Factor a debt which it has already assigned to a third party or, conversely, where the Business assigns to a third party a debt which it has already assigned to the Factor. The general rule in relation to priorities (albeit not without exception) is that where different parties have competing equal interests in the same chose in action, the interest that is created first in time will prevail. However, the general rule in relation to the assignment of debts is different. Where there are two assignees of a debt, priority will be given to the assignee who, having taken the assignment in good faith and without knowledge of any earlier assignment, first gives notice of assignment to the debtor. This is another reason why a Factor who is unable to give notice of assignment by reason of the relevant facility being a confidential one may potentially be disadvantaged.

6-26 In light of the above, it is submitted that where the Factor and the Business enter into a facility which does not restrict notice of assignment, the Factor should ensure that notice is given to the Customer at the earliest possible juncture. In order to satisfy themselves that all invoices are pre-printed/stamped with a notice of assignment, some Factors will require the Business to provide them with copies of all such invoices before they are sent out to the Business's Customers (often by email). Necessarily, however, this can be time-consuming for the Factor and in some circumstances it may not be practical. What the Factor may choose to do instead is to carry out regular audits of the Business's invoices so as to ensure that the

[31] See at 8-18

Business is complying with its contractual obligations as regards providing its Customers with notice of assignment. Additionally, the Factor will usually send out a Welcome Letter to all of the Business's Customers both on the inception of the factoring facility and as and when the Business begins to trade with new Customers. Whilst this may not suffice to ensure valid notice in respect of future invoices[32], it will at least ensure (certainly if sent by email) that the Business's Customers have had notice of assignment in respect of any existing debts owed to the Business.

32 See at 6-13

CHAPTER SEVEN

DEFENCES OF THE CUSTOMER

7-01 In the case of Bibby Factors Northwest Limited v HDF Limited and Another[33], Christopher Clarke LJ set out a useful summary of the ways in which a Customer may defeat the recovery by the Factor of a debt assigned by the Business to the Factor:

> "*An assignee of debts, such as a factor, will seek to recover the whole of the debt assigned. He may fail to do so for at least four reasons. First the debtor may show that the money claimed is not due, in whole or in part, either because of some substantive defence or some right of abatement. Second, the debtor may have a contractual right of set off. Third, the debtor may have a cross claim which equity will regard him as entitled to set off against the debt such that only the balance may be claimed. If so, and subject to any question of estoppel, the factor, as assignee, can be in no better position than his assignor, whether the assignment takes effect as a statutory assignment or in equity. It is no matter that the cross claim had not accrued due before the debtor had notice of the assignment. Fourth, the debtor may have a cross claim which is independent of the claim against him in the sense that it does not fall into the category of a claim which forms the subject of an equitable set off. In such a case the factor/assignee cannot successfully be met by a cross claim*

[33] [2015] EWCA Civ 1908

which arose after the Customer/debtor had notice of the assignment."

Substantive Defence

7-02 The general rule is that a debtor may set up against the assignee of the debt any defence he could have raised against the assignor of the debt: this is because the assignee cannot stand in better shoes than the assignor vis-à-vis his ability to recover the assigned debt from the debtor. So, for example, if the Business has raised and assigned to the Factor an invoice in respect of goods which it failed to deliver to the Customer, the Customer can raise against the Factor a defence under section 51 of the Sale of Goods Act 1979 and/or a defence of total failure of consideration. Equally, if the Customer was (for example) induced to purchase goods from the Business by reason of an actionable misrepresentation on the part of the Business, the Customer will be able to raise this as a defence to any claim brought by the Factor for non-payment of the invoices to which the goods relate.

Abatement

7-03 The common law remedy of abatement is derived from the decision in *Mondel v Steel*[34]. As per Lord Diplock at 717 in the case of *Gilbert-Ash (Northern) Ltd v Modern Engineering (Bristol) Ltd*[35] abatement is:

> *"... a remedy which the common law provides for breaches of warranty in contracts for sale of goods and for work and labour. It is restricted to contracts of these types. It is*

---

34 151 E.R. 1288

35 [1974] A.C. 689

available as of right to a party to such a contract. It does not lie within the discretion of the court to withhold it. It is independent of the doctrine of 'equitable set off' "

7-04 In the case of contracts for the sale of goods, the common law remedy of abatement is enshrined in section 53(1)(a) of the Sale of Goods Act 1979 which provides that:

> "*Where there is a breach of warranty by the seller, or where the buyer elects (or is compelled) to treat any breach of a condition on the part of the seller as a breach of warranty, the buyer is not by reason only of such breach of warranty entitled to reject the goods; but he may.....set up against the seller the breach of warranty in diminution or extinction of the price.*"

7-05 Given that abatement is (strictly speaking) a defence in its own right, a Customer who would have been able to assert a right of abatement as a defence to a claim by the Business for non-payment of the Business's invoice will also be able to assert the same right against the Factor as assignee of the Business's invoice.

SET-OFF

7-06 In the context of factoring, a right of set-off is the right of a Customer to reduce or extinguish the debt it owes the Factor by reason of a countervailing right the Customer has against the Business for a monetary sum.

7-07 As stated above, the general rule is that the assignee of a debt cannot stand in better shoes than the assignor of the debt. In other words, if the debtor would have had a defence of set-off against the assignor had the debt not been assigned to the assignee, he can (subject to certain qualifications) raise the same defence of set-off against the assignee.

Types of Set-Off

7-08 Broadly speaking, there are four categories of set-off which are relevant in the context of factoring:

i. Statutory/Independent set-off;

ii. Equitable set-off;

iii. Contractual set-off;

iv. Insolvency set-off.

Statutory/Independent Set-Off

7-09 Statutory set-off (commonly known as 'Independent' set-off) is a procedural right (rather than a legal one) which only arises in the context of litigation. Historically, it has been called 'statutory' set-off because it has its origins in the Statutes of Set Off[36] (now repealed) which provided, in terms, that a defendant to a claim for the payment of money could set off against that claim any mutual monetary claim he might have against the claimant.

7-10 The reason why this category of set-off is now more commonly known as 'independent' set-off is because there need not be any factual or legal connection between the claimant's claim and the defendant's cross-claim – i.e. they need not arise out of the same transaction or even a linked transaction. They can

36 Insolvent Debtors Relief Act 1929 & Debtors Relief (Amendment) Act 1735

be completely unrelated and wholly independent of one another. As stated by Lord Hoffman in Stein v Blake[37]:

> "*Legal set-off does not affect the substantive rights of the parties against each other, at any rate until both causes of action have been merged in a judgment of the court. It addresses questions of procedure and cash-flow. As a matter of procedure, it enables a Defendant to require his cross-claim (even if based upon a wholly different subject matter) to be tried together with the Plaintiff's claim instead of having to be the subject of a separate action. In this way it ensures that judgment will be given simultaneously on claim and cross-claim and thereby relieves the defendant from having to find the cash to satisfy a judgment in favour of the plaintiff (or, in the 18th century, go to a debtor's prison) before his cross-claim has been determined.*"

7-11 In order to establish an independent set-off, the defendant will need to demonstrate that the following criteria are satisfied:

i. Both the claim and the cross-claim are between the same parties and in the same capacity, right or interest;

ii. Both the claim and the cross-claim are for liquidated sums or sums capable of being readily ascertained;

iii. The sum which the defendant is seeking to set off is due, owing and enforceable by way of suit at the time the defendant pleads his defence;

37 [1996] A.C. 243 at 251

iv. The sum which the defendant is seeking to set off also remains due and owing at the date of trial.

7-12 In the context of factoring, a Customer presented with a claim by a Factor for payment of an assigned invoice can raise a defence of independent set-off against the Factor provided that: 1) the aforesaid criteria are satisfied; and 2) the debt or other cause of action giving rise to the set-off had accrued prior to the date on which the Customer was given notice of assignment.

7-13 It is important to note that a debt which accrues after the date on which notice of assignment was given to the Customer cannot be the subject of an independent set-off (even if it arises out a contract which pre-dates the notice of assignment). Conversely, however, a debt which has not become payable as at the date of notice of assignment can still be the subject of an independent set-off so long as the Customer's right to future payment had accrued prior to the date of notice of assignment.

Equitable Set-Off

7-14 As its name suggests, equitable set-off (sometimes known as 'Transactional' set-off) has its origins in equity rather than statute. The modern concept of equitable set-off is generally considered to derive from the case of Hanak v Green.[38] However, the accepted test for equitable set-off is now that stated by Rix LJ in Geldof Metaalconstructie NV v Simon Carves Limited[39]: it arises where a debtor has a cross-claim "*so closely connected with [the creditor's] demands that it would be*

[38] [1958] 2 QB9

[39] [2010] EWCA Civ 667

manifestly unjust to allow him to enforce payment without taking into account the cross-claim".

7-15 Whereas independent set-off can only arise in the context of litigation, equitable set-off is a self-help remedy available to the debtor even where there is no litigation pending or in contemplation. Equally, whilst it is a requirement for independent set-off that both the claim and the cross-claim are for liquidated sums or sums that are readily ascertainable, this is not a requirement for equitable set-off. It seems that where a debtor has a cross-claim for unliquidated damages, he may set this off against the creditor's claim by deducting a reasonable assessment of his loss made in good faith.[40]

7-16 In contrast to the position of a Customer relying on independent set-off, a Customer seeking to rely on equitable set-off need not show that it has a cross-claim which arises from a cause of action which accrued prior to notice of assignment. Provided that there is a sufficiently close nexus between the assigned invoice in respect of which the Factor is seeking payment and the subject-matter of the Customer's cross-claim, the date on which notice of assignment was given to the Customer is generally irrelevant[41].

7-17 So, in the context of factoring, a Customer presented with a claim by a Factor for payment of an assigned invoice can, generally speaking, raise a defence of equitable set-off against the Factor where it can demonstrate that it has a cross-claim against the Business (whether for a liquidated or an unliquidated sum) which arises out of the same transaction as

---

40 The Nanfri – [1978] Q.B. 927_

41 Business Computers Ltd v Anglo-African Leasing Ltd [1977] 1 W.L.R. 578, 585;

the assigned invoice or arises out of a transaction which is so closely connected with the transaction from which the assigned invoice arises that it would be manifestly unjust to allow the Factor to enforce payment of the assigned invoice without taking into account the Customer's cross-claim. If the Customer can establish this, it matters not when notice of assignment was received by the Customer.

7-18 Where a Business sells goods to a Customer and those goods turn out to be defective, the Customer may have a claim for damages against the Business for breach of warranty which it can offset against the invoice raised by the Business for the price of the goods. If the Business assigns the invoice to a Factor and the Factor seeks to recover payment of the invoice from the Customer, the Customer will be able to raise the same defence of equitable set-off against the Factor. This is relatively straightforward because the Customer's cross-claim arises out of the same transaction as the invoice and the claim and the cross-claim are obviously connected.

7-19 Where the Customer's cross-claim does not arise out of the same transaction as the assigned invoice, it will be necessary for the Customer to establish that its cross-claim arises from a transaction which is so closely connected to the transaction giving rise to the assigned invoice that it would be manifestly unjust for the Factor to enforce payment of the assigned invoice without taking into account the Customer's cross-claim. What amounts to a sufficiently close connection between the claim and the cross-claim that it would be "*manifestly unjust*" to allow enforcement of the claim without taking into account the cross-claim is not always so straightforward to determine.

7-20 In the case of Bibby Factors Northwest Limited v HDF Limited and Another[42], the Customer asserted that it had an equitable set off against the invoices assigned by the Business to the Factor on the basis that it was entitled to a rebate from the Business of 10% of the price payable by the Customer for every supply made in a given calendar year. At trial, the Factor conceded that there was a close connection between the assigned invoices and the Customer's cross-claim to a rebate but argued that there would be no manifest injustice in allowing the Factor to recover on the claim without having regard to the cross-claim. This was because, although the Customer knew that the Factor had taken an assignment of the debts owed by the Customer to the Business, the Customer never brought the rebate arrangement to the Factor's attention despite the fact (inter alia) that a sticker had been affixed to each of the Business's invoices before they were sent to the Customer stating that: "*[the Factor] alone can give a valid discharge and should be advised immediately of any dispute likely to defer payment beyond terms of sale* ".

7-21 The Judge at first instance concluded that there was no contractual or other obligation on the Customer to inform the Factor of the existence of the rebate and he was satisfied that the claim to the rebate was so closely connected with the Factor's demand that it would be manifestly unjust to allow the Factor to enforce payment without taking account of the rebate cross claim. If the Business had brought an action against the Customer for payment of invoices, the Customer would have been entitled to set off the sums due on the rebate and the Factor could be in no better position. The judge was

[42] [2015] EWCA Civ 1908

fortified in his conclusion because he considered that the claim and cross claim almost certainly arose out of the same contract.

7-22 On appeal, the Factor argued that in reaching his conclusions regarding the proximity between the claim and the cross-claim, the Judge at first instance had failed to take into account "*the justice of the case*" and that if he had taken this into account, he would have concluded that the link between the claim and the cross-claim was not sufficient to justify a set-off. Christopher Clark LJ disagreed, stating at [48]:

> "*The relevant exercise is not a general decision as to the justice of the case. The question is whether the connection between the claim by [the Business] and the cross claim by the Customer is so close that it would be unjust to allow [the Business] (and hence [the Factor]) to maintain the one without giving credit to the Customer for the other. The putative victim of such injustice is the debtor. On that question the answer is, in my view, plainly in the affirmative. It does not seem to me, any more than it did to the judge [39], that the action or inaction of [the Customer] towards [the Factor] can, in the present case, sever the link.*"

Contractual Set-Off

7-23 Contractual set-off arises from the contractual terms expressly agreed by parties in relation to their respective rights of set-off against one another. Such terms can be used to augment the rights of set-off (i.e. to provide that one or both of the parties will have additional rights of set-off beyond those which they would normally have against one another) or they can be used to limit or exclude such rights altogether.

7-24 It is common in commercial contracts for a party supplying goods or services to include within its standard terms and conditions a clause dictating that the paying party to the contract will pay the sums due for the goods or services in full and without recourse to any right of set-off. The purpose of this is to ensure that the supplier's cashflow is maintained and it does not have to await the outcome of a dispute raised by the other party before receiving payment[43].

7-25 The existence of an effective no set-off clause in a Business's terms and conditions is something which an astute Factor will be keen to ensure. Indeed, some Factors may insist on the existence of such a clause before entering into a facility with a Business. If the Customer would be prevented from setting up a right of set-off against the Business, it will be prevented from doing so against the Factor. This means that the Factor should receive full payment of the assigned invoice and the Customer is left to pursue its dispute directly against the Business.

7-26 It is important to bear in mind, however, that where the contract between the Business and the Customer is governed by the Business's standard terms and conditions, any no set-off clause contained in those terms and conditions may be vulnerable to challenge on grounds of reasonableness under the Unfair Contract Terms Act 1977. Equally, it is important to note that any no set-off clause agreed between the parties

[43] See Venson Automotive Solutions Ltd v Morrison's Facilities Services Ltd, Manchester Working Ltd, Mears Scotland LLP, Mears Scotland (Services) Ltd [2019] EWHC 3089 (Comm)

(however widely drafted) is incapable of excluding insolvency set-off.[44]

7-27 In the case of contracts of carriage (by sea, air and road), set-off is prohibited (with or without an express no set-off clause) by reason of the decision in Aries Tanker Corp v Total Transport Ltd.[45]

Insolvency Set-Off

7-28 Insolvency set-off arises automatically by operation of section 323 of the Insolvency Act 1986 (in the case of bankruptcy) and rules 14.24 and 14.25 of the Insolvency Rules 2016 (in the case of liquidation and administration). These provisions mandate that where a debtor has (prior to becoming insolvent) had mutual dealings with a creditor whereby there are sums due from the debtor to the creditor and from the creditor to the debtor, an account must be taken of what is owed by each of them and the resulting sums must be set off against each other. If, after an account has been taken, there is a sum which remains due and owing to the creditor from the insolvent debtor, this is the sum in respect of which the creditor may prove in the bankruptcy/winding up. Conversely, if, after an account has been taken, there is a sum which remains due and owing from the creditor to the insolvent debtor, it will be this sum which is payable by the creditor to the trustee in bankruptcy/administrator/liquidator. Insolvency set-off is mandatory and parties cannot agree to contract out of it or exercise any right of waiver.

---

44 National Westminster Bank Ltd v Halesowen Presswork & Assemblies Ltd [1972] A.C. 785.

45 (The Aries) [1977] 1 All E.R. 398

7-29 Because insolvency set-off operates on the basis of mutuality of dealings between an insolvent debtor and his creditor, the assignee of a debt owed by the insolvent debtor to the creditor will not be affected by insolvency set-off, there being no mutuality of dealings between the assignee and the insolvent debtor. In the context of factoring, therefore, this means that the debt assigned to the Factor by the Business is not *automatically* set-off against sums owed by the Business to the insolvent Customer even though there may have been mutual dealings between the insolvent Customer and the Business which would otherwise be subject to insolvency set-off. However, an insolvent Customer can still rely on independent or equitable set-off as a defence whereby it can reduce or extinguish the amount owed to the Factor. If an insolvent debtor is unable to rely on either of these defences against the Factor, it still has the ability to pursue the Business for any sums to which it is entitled from the Business.

CHAPTER EIGHT

LITIGATION

8-01 The majority of factoring facilities operate effectively and harmoniously to the mutual benefit of both the Factor and the Business. As in all areas of commerce, however, disputes do arise from time to time and sometimes those disputes result in litigation. There are certain issues which arise frequently in such litigation and which are, consequently, worthy of discussion.

GUARANTORS

8-02 Claims by Factors against Guarantors account for a significant amount of the litigation undertaken in the arena of factoring. This is perhaps unsurprising given that the majority of Businesses with whom the Factor will contract are limited companies which can and often do become insolvent, leaving the Factor only with the benefit of any securities it has obtained over the assets of the Business and/or with the right to call upon those individuals/companies from whom it has obtained guarantees and indemnities.

8-03 Whilst the majority of Guarantors will (insofar as they are able to do so) defend proceedings on the basis of defences which the Business may have been able to raise against the Factor, a defence which is raised with reasonable frequency by individual personal Guarantors is that they either did not sign the guarantee at all (and hence the signature on the guarantee is a forgery perpetrated by the Factor) or that when signing the guarantee they did not know and/or understand what they were signing.

8-04 Whilst, in the majority of cases, it is reasonably clear that the Guarantor did sign the relevant document, the mere assertion of fraud by the Guarantor can give the Court cause for concern and make it difficult for the Factor to obtain judgment against a Guarantor otherwise than after a fully contested trial wherein the Court hears oral evidence from both parties and (in some cases) from a hand-writing expert. Necessarily, this is frustrating and potentially expensive for a Factor who would, in an ideal world, apply for summary judgment on what is an otherwise undisputed debt.

8-05 It is not uncommon for a Guarantor defending a claim brought by a Factor to assert that he was never asked to sign a guarantee and that the first time he ever saw a copy of it was when the Factor first demanded payment from him. There are a number of potential steps a Factor can take to protect itself against an assertion of this nature.

8-06 In the first instance, a typical written factoring agreement will usually specify on its face what securities the Factor requires before it will advance any monies to the Business. Where such securities include a guarantee and indemnity from an individual who is a director/designated partner of the Business, the relevant Guarantor will usually be identified by name. In and of itself, this tends to cast significant doubt on a Guarantor's assertion that he was never asked to sign a guarantee and knew nothing about it until a demand was made of him by the Factor. Given that the individuals commonly asked to provide guarantees to the Factor tend to be critically involved with the Business at an operational level, it is more than likely that they will also be signatories to the factoring agreement in their capacity as agents of the Business. In the circumstances, they will be deemed to have read the factoring agreement before signing it and before signing the guarantee and the suggestion that they were unaware that a guarantee was required of them before demand for payment was made by the Factor necessarily tends to lack credibility.

8-07 In addition to explicitly naming the Guarantor on the face of the factoring agreement, many Factors will also ensure that prior to the Guarantor signing the guarantee, an unexecuted copy of it has been sent to him by email (together with a copy of the written factoring agreement and an explanation of what the guarantee entails). Likewise, some Factors will take the precaution of emailing a copy of the executed guarantee to the Guarantor shortly after he has signed it. If documents are sent to the Guarantor only by post or presented to the Guarantor only during an unrecorded face to face meeting, there is significantly more scope for the Guarantor to deny either that he ever received it or that he signed it. This is particularly so where the representative of the Factor who conducted the introductory meeting with the Business and the Guarantor has left the employment of the Factor or is otherwise unable to recall the specific meeting. Conversely, if a signed copy of the guarantee executed by the Guarantor is sent to him by email shortly after execution and he doesn't raise any query in response, it will be significantly harder for him to challenge its authenticity.

8-08 Equally, Factors wishing to dispel the assertion that the Guarantor did not understand what he was signing will frequently ensure that the Guarantor signs a document confirming that, prior to signing the guarantee, he had fully read and understood its terms and effect and that he had been given the opportunity to seek legal advice in respect of it.

Whilst is not unknown for a Guarantor also to dispute the authenticity of this document, it at least adds a layer of protection for the Factor, especially if the Factor can evidence that that Guarantor was contemporaneously provided with a signed copy of the document by email and that he did not query it.

8-09 Another potential issue which can arise in the context of litigation against Guarantors is an assertion by the Guarantor that the sums for which he is being sued fall outside the scope of his guarantee. For example, where a Guarantor has provided a guarantee and indemnity in the context of a non-recourse factoring agreement entered into by the Factor and the Business and the Factor and the Business subsequently agree to replace that agreement with a recourse facility, it may be argued by the Guarantor that any sums due and owing to the Factor under the terms of the new recourse facility fall outside the scope of what he originally agreed to guarantee, the financial risks to the Business being significantly greater under a recourse facility than a non-recourse facility. Whilst one would hope that such an eventuality would be caught by a sufficiently widely drafted definition of 'Guaranteed Obligations', it is submitted that as a matter of good practice, a Factor should require the Guarantor to execute a new guarantee in the event that there is a substantial variation to/wholesale replacement of the facility in respect of which the original guarantee was signed.

NOTICE OF ASSIGNMENT

8-10 In litigation brought by the Factor against the Business's Customer, one of the most frequently raised defences is that the Customer never received notice of the assignment by the Business to the Factor of the claimed invoices. If the Factor has sued in its own name, without joining the Business to the proceedings, many Customers argue that the absence of a valid notice of assignment renders the litigation defective (or sometimes even abortive). This is because the absence of a valid notice of assignment renders the assignment one which take places in equity only and the Factor therefore needs to ensure that the assignor of the debt (i.e. the Business) is joined into any proceedings against the Customer.

8-11 For the reasons stated above[46], this argument is generally misconceived. To avoid such an argument even being raised, however, the Factor will want to do all that it can to ensure that it can evidence that notice of assignment was provided to the Customer[47].

QUANTIFICATION

8-12 A significant proportion of the litigation brought by Factors against Businesses and/or Guarantors is defended on the basis that the Business/Guarantor does not accept the Factor's quantification of the amounts the Factor claims to be owed.

8-13 To mitigate against a defence of this nature, almost all well-drafted factoring agreements and guarantees will contain terms

---

46 See at 6-16 to 6-18

47 See at 6-26

whereby the Business/Guarantor is deemed to accept that a written certificate which evidences the amount of the Business's/Guarantor's liability to the Factor, and which has been signed either by the Factor's company secretary or by a director of the Factor, is conclusive and binding on the Business/Guarantor (save in the case of manifest error).

8-14 In practice, these clauses are effective where the Business and/or Guarantor asserts that it/he is not liable to make payment to the Factor until such time as the Factor has provided accounting records to show that each and every pound and penny the Factor has claimed is due and owing by the Business/Guarantor. Vague denials and defences where the Business/Guarantor simply puts the Factor to proof of the sums owed will often fall foul of such clauses on an application by the Factor for summary judgment. Experience dictates, however, that where the Business/Guarantor can evidence even a minor error in the Factor's accounting, such clauses are unlikely to carry the day for the Factor. Instead, it is likely that the Factor will have to prove, by reference to accounting data, the exact figure it claims to be owed by the Business and how that figure has been calculated: a certificate signed by the company secretary or a director of the Factor will not suffice.

DISCHARGE OF CUSTOMER

8-17 Whilst the majority of Businesses will abide by their contractual and fiduciary duties to the Factor, it is not unheard of for a Business with the benefit of a disclosed factoring agreement secretly to try and persuade its Customers not to make payment to the Factor (as required by the notice of assignment provided to the Customer) but instead to make payment directly to the Business.

8-18 Some Customers, often acting in good faith and in ignorance of the implications of their actions, will do as the Business requests and make payment of an assigned debt directly to the Business. When the Factor discovers this and intimates a claim against the Customer for payment of the debt, the Customer argues that it has already paid the debt and should not have to pay any further sums to the Factor. However, provided the Customer has had notice of assignment before it pays the debt to the Business, it will not be discharged from its liability to the Factor. Authority for this principle is derived from the case of William Brandt's Sons & Co. v Dunlop Rubber Company Limited[48] where Lord Macnaghten stated at 461:

> "*Then the Dunlops receive through Brandts a notice which no man of business could mistake, telling them, on Kramrisch & Co.'s express authority, that they are to pay to Brandts the money which they owe their creditors, Kramrisch & Co. What more could be required? Dunlops disregard that notice and pay the wrong people. They must pay the money over again and pay it to the right person.*"

8-19 Whilst the fact that the Customer has to pay again may, at first blush, seem draconian (especially where the Customer was deceived or coerced by the Business into making payment to the Business rather than the Factor), the reality of the situation is that the Customer disregards a notice of assignment at its own peril. A Factor may choose whether or not to protect its interests by giving notice of assignment to the Customer. If the Factor chooses not to give notice of assignment, it must accept the consequences of this. Conversely, if it does choose to protect its interests by giving notice of assignment, it is entitled to reap the benefits of that choice. It should not be forgotten,

[48] [1905] A.C. 454

as well, that the Customer will usually have a restitutionary claim against the Business for repayment of the monies it paid to the Business in respect of the relevant invoice(s).

MORE BOOKS BY LAW BRIEF PUBLISHING

A selection of our other titles available now:-

'A Practical Guide to the Independent School Standards – September 2023 Edition' by Sarah McKimm
'A Practical Guide to Estate Administration and Crypto Assets' by Richard Marshall
'A Practical Guide to Managing GDPR Data Subject Access Requests – Second Edition' by Patrick O'Kane
'A Practical Guide to Parental Alienation in Private and Public Law Children Cases' by Sam King QC & Frankie Shama
'Contested Heritage – Removing Art from Land and Historic Buildings' by Richard Harwood QC, Catherine Dobson, David Sawtell
'The Limits of Separate Legal Personality: When Those Running a Company Can Be Held Personally Liable for Losses Caused to Third Parties Outside of the Company' by Dr Mike Wilkinson
'A Practical Guide to Transgender Law' by Robin Moira White & Nicola Newbegin
'A Practical Guide to 'Stranded Spouses' in Family Law' by Mani Singh Basi
'A Practical Guide to Residential Freehold Conveyancing' by Lorraine Richardson
'A Practical Guide to Pensions on Divorce for Lawyers' by Bryan Scant
'A Practical Guide to Challenging Sham Marriage Allegations in Immigration Law' by Priya Solanki
'A Practical Guide to Digital Communications Evidence in Criminal Law' by Sam Willis
'A Practical Guide to Legal Rights in Scotland' by Sarah-Jane Macdonald
'A Practical Guide to New Build Conveyancing' by Paul Sams & Rebecca East
'A Practical Guide to Defending Barristers in Disciplinary Cases' by Marc Beaumont
'A Practical Guide to Inherited Wealth on Divorce' by Hayley Trim
'A Practical Guide to Practice Direction 12J and Domestic Abuse in Private Law Children Proceedings' by Rebecca Cross & Malvika Jaganmohan

'A Practical Guide to Confiscation and Restraint' by Narita Bahra QC, John Carl Townsend, David Winch
'A Practical Guide to the Law of Forests in Scotland' by Philip Buchan
'A Practical Guide to Health and Medical Cases in Immigration Law' by Rebecca Chapman & Miranda Butler
'A Practical Guide to Bad Character Evidence for Criminal Practitioners by Aparna Rao
'A Practical Guide to Extradition Law post-Brexit' by Myles Grandison et al
'A Practical Guide to Hoarding and Mental Health for Housing Lawyers' by Rachel Coyle
'A Practical Guide to Psychiatric Claims in Personal Injury – 2nd Edition' by Liam Ryan
'Stephens on Contractual Indemnities' by Richard Stephens
'A Practical Guide to the EU Succession Regulation' by Richard Frimston
'A Practical Guide to Solicitor and Client Costs – 2nd Edition' by Robin Dunne
'Constructive Dismissal – Practice Pointers and Principles' by Benjimin Burgher
'A Practical Guide to Religion and Belief Discrimination Claims in the Workplace' by Kashif Ali
'A Practical Guide to the Law of Medical Treatment Decisions' by Ben Troke
'Fundamental Dishonesty and QOCS in Personal Injury Proceedings: Law and Practice' by Jake Rowley
'A Practical Guide to the Law in Relation to School Exclusions' by Charlotte Hadfield & Alice de Coverley
'A Practical Guide to Divorce for the Silver Separators' by Karin Walker
'The Right to be Forgotten – The Law and Practical Issues' by Melissa Stock
'A Practical Guide to Planning Law and Rights of Way in National Parks, the Broads and AONBs' by James Maurici QC, James Neill et al
'A Practical Guide to Election Law' by Tom Tabori
'A Practical Guide to the Law in Relation to Surrogacy' by Andrew Powell
'A Practical Guide to Claims Arising from Fatal Accidents – 2nd Edition' by James Patience
'A Practical Guide to the Ownership of Employee Inventions – From Entitlement to Compensation' by James Tumbridge & Ashley Roughton
'A Practical Guide to Asbestos Claims' by Jonathan Owen & Gareth McAloon

'A Practical Guide to Stamp Duty Land Tax in England and Northern Ireland' by Suzanne O'Hara
'A Practical Guide to the Law of Farming Partnerships' by Philip Whitcomb
'Covid-19, Homeworking and the Law – The Essential Guide to Employment and GDPR Issues' by Forbes Solicitors
'Covid-19 and Criminal Law – The Essential Guide' by Ramya Nagesh
'Covid-19 and Family Law in England and Wales – The Essential Guide' by Safda Mahmood
'A Practical Guide to the Law of Unlawful Eviction and Harassment – 2nd Edition' by Stephanie Lovegrove
'Covid-19, Brexit and the Law of Commercial Leases – The Essential Guide' by Mark Shelton
'A Practical Guide to Costs in Personal Injury Claims – 2nd Edition' by Matthew Hoe
'A Practical Guide to the General Data Protection Regulation (GDPR) – 2nd Edition' by Keith Markham
'Ellis on Credit Hire – Sixth Edition' by Aidan Ellis & Tim Kevan
'A Practical Guide to Working with Litigants in Person and McKenzie Friends in Family Cases' by Stuart Barlow
'Protecting Unregistered Brands: A Practical Guide to the Law of Passing Off' by Lorna Brazell
'A Practical Guide to Secondary Liability and Joint Enterprise Post-Jogee' by Joanne Cecil & James Mehigan
'A Practical Guide to the Pre-Action RTA Claims Protocol for Personal Injury Lawyers' by Antonia Ford
'A Practical Guide to Neighbour Disputes and the Law' by Alexander Walsh
'A Practical Guide to Forfeiture of Leases' by Mark Shelton
'A Practical Guide to Coercive Control for Legal Practitioners and Victims' by Rachel Horman
'A Practical Guide to the Law of Driverless Cars – Second Edition' by Alex Glassbrook, Emma Northey & Scarlett Milligan
'A Practical Guide to TOLATA Claims' by Greg Williams
'A Practical Guide to Elderly Law – 2nd Edition' by Justin Patten
'A Practical Guide to Responding to Housing Disrepair and Unfitness Claims' by Iain Wightwick

'A Practical Guide to the Law of Bullying and Harassment in the Workplace' by Philip Hyland
'How to Be a Freelance Solicitor: A Practical Guide to the SRA-Regulated Freelance Solicitor Model' by Paul Bennett
'A Practical Guide to Prison Injury Claims' by Malcolm Johnson
'A Practical Guide to the Small Claims Track – 2nd Edition' by Dominic Bright
'A Practical Guide to Advising Clients at the Police Station' by Colin Stephen McKeown-Beaumont
'A Practical Guide to Antisocial Behaviour Injunctions' by Iain Wightwick
'Practical Mediation: A Guide for Mediators, Advocates, Advisers, Lawyers, and Students in Civil, Commercial, Business, Property, Workplace, and Employment Cases' by Jonathan Dingle with John Sephton
'The Mini-Pupillage Workbook' by David Boyle
'A Practical Guide to Crofting Law' by Brian Inkster
'A Practical Guide to the Law of Domain Names and Cybersquatting' by Andrew Clemson
'A Practical Guide to the Law of Gender Pay Gap Reporting' by Harini Iyengar
'NHS Whistleblowing and the Law' by Joseph England
'Employment Law and the Gig Economy' by Nigel Mackay & Annie Powell
'A Practical Guide to Noise Induced Hearing Loss (NIHL) Claims' by Andrew Mckie, Ian Skeate, Gareth McAloon
'An Introduction to Beauty Negligence Claims – A Practical Guide for the Personal Injury Practitioner' by Greg Almond
'Intercompany Agreements for Transfer Pricing Compliance' by Paul Sutton
'Zen and the Art of Mediation' by Martin Plowman
'A Practical Guide to the SRA Principles, Individual and Law Firm Codes of Conduct 2019 – What Every Law Firm Needs to Know' by Paul Bennett
'A Practical Guide to Adoption for Family Lawyers' by Graham Pegg
'A Practical Guide to Industrial Disease Claims' by Andrew Mckie & Ian Skeate
'A Practical Guide to Redundancy' by Philip Hyland
'A Practical Guide to Vicarious Liability' by Mariel Irvine
'A Practical Guide to Applications for Landlord's Consent and Variation of Leases' by Mark Shelton
'A Practical Guide to Relief from Sanctions Post-Mitchell and Denton' by Peter Causton

www.ingramcontent.com/pod-product-compliance
Lightning Source LLC
LaVergne TN
LVHW022305200926
848481LV00004B/1222